D1097748

Eirenikon

Also by Gavin Bantock

Christ   *1965*
Juggernaut   *1968*
A New Thing Breathing   *1969*
Anhaga   *1972*
Gleeman   *1972*

EIRENIKON

A poem by Gavin Bantock

Anvil Press Poetry
associated with
Routledge & Kegan Paul

First published in 1972
by Anvil Press Poetry
69 King George Street London SE10 8PX
Distributed by Routledge & Kegan Paul Ltd

Clothbound SBN 900977–87–6
Paperbound SBN 900977–88–4

A limited edition of fifty numbered copies have been specially bound
and signed by the author
SBN 900977–89–2

Printed in Great Britain by
The Bowering Press Plymouth

to

Masayuki Okada
Hidetoshi Kawabe
&
Sajio Takemasa

who proved that it is possible

EIRENIKON

A proposition, scheme or treatise designed to promote peace

PROPOSITION

(a) A formal statement of a theorem or problem, often including the demonstration

(b) 'A form of words which expresses what is either true or false' (Bertrand Russell)

'The whole is greater than the part' (Euclid)

Given

collision of surd and abacus

To prove

that quietude may be something akin to a green fern
a man can carry with him in his hands
unfading until the end of the world

Given

anarchy
thrown to the winds blowing within the twenty-four
right-angles set in a white box

and

mathematics
coined and commissioned to design one
fugue from the rulerless dimensions of the nightly
journeying spaces between the stars

given
collapsed rainbows reminiscent of vomited candy
given
doves foaming at the mouth over dead waters

given
sunless plateaux littered with gods dying of leukaemia

given
the mind-stunning
sound of echelons of obsolete bomber-squadrons
all day long tattooing the overhead wind

given
the worn-down
dynamoes under the assembly-lines of the white-flag-flying
armament factories in the mountains of Kamchatka

given
nicotine-stained eyeballs
given

widdershin spores gnawing at the core of the bones
given
fibrillating ribcages blue-black with a plethora of anti-biotics

given
adolescents
dying of old age

given
dead-weight catalogues of tenement-dwellers
constantly on the move
given
the impossibility of true solitude in ghetto
saucepans full of maggots boiling without water on gas-rings

given
trees
that excel mildew only in size

given
flowers
made of plastic because they look more real on television
stared at after supper by families sitting
slippered in their shock-deadening armchairs

given
smiling newscasters reading from smoothly-digested
novels with honey pouring from their rosy mouths
given
naked black scorpion-minded headlines glanced at once and at once
torn up and used to light bonfires in back-gardens at weekends

given paradise
                a divine
two-week holiday in Majorca on a charter-flight package-tour
or laughter on close-cropped lawns and men

diving into an empty swimming pool

given hell
            an overwhelmingly
easy journey with commuters in a train
passing by endless telegraph poles and lines of wires silently
or hooded crones murmuring again and again the terror of having
no telephones in hell

given
love-making rendered cripple or criminal or totally
null and sensation-empty by depraved vikings
lifting their mauve loaded minds out into the cleanest
streets in the world

given
the doll boredom where there are no known
fissures in the porcelain face of the world

given
a surfeit of spirit-levels and waters
calmed by the oil bulk of incontinent tankers
poster-yellow beaches designed for anatomy funfairs
bedevilled by the cries of tar-skinned gannets
oceans pregnant with gomulka heavy green
gravy and bubbles eased up from dead mermaids
indestructible plastic cleanser bottles
blighting the skull-and-crossbone findings of mudlarks
and
whales dying of the spewed excrement of company directors

given
computers programmed only to calculate
the multiples of malignant cancer cells
lodged in the mouthpieces of trombones

given
power stations half-dazed by cerebral strokes
paralysing the right sides of industrial towns

given
dilapidated bill-boards everywhere proclaiming that
America leads the liberty and the peace
and the longest-lasting bilge of the world

given
the mad Pope in a leaking chastity belt
flying by jet to raise his frail jewel-dispensing white
arms in hot countries where jewel-bedecked churches
look down on acres of tin shacks cut off from Jesus
as surely as Christ is cut off from the black
pebbles which shine in the ponds of Japanese eyes

given
jungles, even those in Sumatra, or the blue
domes of Samarkand, or the straits of Magellan
all echoing with the panic of tottering
moguls and demagogues hammering nails into the steel
golgothas of tomorrow

given
heads of state who have no heads for heights
save to push buttons to save the button-makers
and to scream down golden telephones

given
god who above all
made a desert and called it peace

given
god as one who has

given
this god-given, god-blessed, god-damned
little round blue world

It is required to prove

peace can be some thing

other than a seven-flavoured mirage
spanning the cadmium clouds over desert cities

other than a bewildered, meandering dove
lifting a dead crow across seas of ceasefires

other than lambs' wool caught on the barbed wire
people use to tie up their christmas presents with

other than a party game for the top ten
played with a brand-new stylus and a worn-out record

other than doctrines and conundrums
crooned in half-empty conference halls
or jargon of promised lands

it is required to prove that
the black clouds rising beyond the tragic
greek mouth of a child
when bombers drop down dead in no man's land
can be annihilated

        to prove that
knowledge of the long-suffering sun's ulcers and convulsions
screaming through the black nightingale of the cosmos
doesn't lessen the loneliness of two friends
staring at each others' minds and able to see
only the light-years between their outstretched hands

                    to prove that
knowledge of done-in ramshackle stars hardly turning now
can turn the minds of the leaders from academic
cosy preoccupation with palaces and slums
pentagon diagrams of reform and concamerations of power

                    to prove that
setting up life-lines to the banisters of apartment stairs
alone can undermine the concrete origins of tears

                    to prove that
touching with giant steps the smithereen tundras of the
        moon
hasn't damned the fortunes of a Ukraine truck-driver

                    to prove that
man's something more than a brave child growing old

                    to prove that
the blue diamond waters of Baikal needn't die of blindness

                    to prove that
city is possible and that
even Manhattan can stand as a goal in delectable mountains

                    to prove that
a man may dream of and find and then live in and never
        contaminate
somewhere a land like the land before Eden

it is required to prove that
when a black crow hatches from the egg of a white dove
it's not necessarily a battle-bird
heralding the end of the world

it is required to prove that
acts of god and all happenings that necessitate archives
are the executed designs of a kind, thinking god who promised
peace for ever and ever and ever for all men

Construction

Force the rainbow back through its prism
shooting white light again one way

Crucify the dove

Draw a line from the laser eye of man
straight to the yellow tooth of god

Inaugurate the demolition of Babel

Pull down the vampire
ivy from the buttresses of the shining
castles at the edge of the kingdom of heaven

Build air in the castles

Describe a full circle
anywhere and of any circumference
and wash it with clean water

Set out a square
paved with stone blocks one from each nation
and let this be the next world
triumphal with only people there
talking together in quiet voices

Design a set of chessmen and board
using one colour only

Commit pogrom against the occupants of all high-rise buildings
used to catalogue the falling-sickness of cash-registers

Take off the haloes of saints to make them holy

Recrown Delphi
a neglected wisdom tooth is likely to decay

Scrape the mildew off Buddha's eyes

Call Hiroshima and order
the only god whose power has grown with age
to stand by

Mastermind a cathedral out of all the books in the world
so that none can be opened
and worship the open spaces left in gothic libraries

Let there be only one round nation
surrounded by one round blue stormless ocean

Let the tree of knowledge be cursed
fig-leaves and condoms banned

Let the clocks be stopped and turned on
back to the day of the first big bang

Let these things be done or if the desire is stronger
follow the hamelin lemmings into the sea

Proof

The whole earth was of one language

And they said, Let us build a city and a tower
whose top may reach unto heaven
and let us make a name lest we be scattered
abroad upon the face of the whole earth

Now Babel has reached the moon
and language is the splintered diamond of god's voice

Only the cities are of one countenance
sorrow does things even to painted masks

Peace
        is the longest cry but the longest road
leads further back than the strange way
the old man came out of the sea

Peace
        is the longest cry
Any man can think of a way to Eden but none imagine
peace
        is the longest way

A signpost tells you only the ways away
from the one place where it is now
but if a man's thinking of peace he can never
journey anywhere new

Peace was once found in faraway places, but now
skyline roads lead to the well of the world's end
and green landscapes too often looked at turn into

faded photographs of savannah without anacondas

No road, no thoroughfare of ocean
no air-corridor leads anywhere but along
ebony floors towards flawless mirrors

The footsteps of a tank in Sinai are more
easy to follow than those stamped in the moondust by men

And though they stood in the Sea of Storms claiming
   We came in peace
they don't know how to stand up in world halls to speak
   for all mankind

They have healed the hurt of the daughter of my people
lightly, saying
Peace, peace, when there is no

Peace, peace, when there is no war
total enough to warrant peace

Now, we have come here, gentlemen,
to consider the possibilities of considering whether
red-tape can do better than merely delay
the drift of continents or whether
olive-green is the best colour for the new dovecote or what
the best way is to get a hand-hold
to climb a rainbow

Language is a locked room full of front-line
reporters shouting into one telephone

Language is the questions shining in a child's eyes
and an old man tongue-tied with endless
surprise that he was ever born to die

Language is two gangs of tunnel-makers
working from opposite ends towards a common
centre but never meeting inside the mountain

Language is a huge brown toad blinking sometimes on a mudbank

Language is the odyssey along flight-paths of echoes
lost in the acoustics of a sound-room where the only
world-prevailing microphone stands unmanned

And god's face
                is scarred with heathen
And god's mouth
                is a charred mask that once smiled
And god's eyes
                are burnt-out red giants
And god's mind
                is jarring multitudes and deafened stones

Blessed are the poor in spirit
for they can't understand what's going on anywhere

Blessed are they that mourn
for their tears can cool the scorched roads

Blessed are the meek
for it's easier to tell them when to surrender

Blessed are they that hunger and thirst
for they shall be the first to die

Blessed are the merciful
for they can engineer world euthanasia

Blessed are the pure in heart
for they can have their names recorded in the Book of Worms

Blessed are they that have been persecuted
for they can become leaders in underground kingdoms

Blessed are the peacemakers
for they shall be called the Sons of God

They shall endure his constant
dissatisfaction with the world he made for a plaything

They shall listen to his kind
scorn damning and damaging their writhing lands

They shall hear and obey with fair minds
the left-wing flutters of the man at his right hand

They shall thank him for the abundant
vicissitudes of his winter winds

Blessed are the Sons of God
for they shall be called peacemakers

They shall be called the newsflash
pacemakers of fashionable escape-routes

They shall bear mongols with cracked tongues
they shall inherit the treasures of madhouses
they shall suffer the landslide victories of acts of god
they shall march in the epidemic vanguards
fingering the bedsores on the whites of their eyes
they shall seek the mainline lanes to valhalla
but on the way there get shot in an underground train
they shall instruct sodom and gomorrah
how to preach the divine birth of gonorrhea

Blessed are the makers of peace

Blessed are ye when men shall reproach you
for you can go to church on Sundays

Blessed are ye when men shall persecute you
for you can put some new pence in the collection box

Blessed are ye when men shall say
all manner of evil against you falsely
for you can say the same things in private
when you go to break wind in the confession box

Rejoice and be exceeding glad for great is your reward
surely his goodness and mercy shall grant you
a cup of tea and a biscuit in the interval

There is no peace unto the wicked, saith the lord
There is no peace, saith the lord unto the wicked
There is no peace

Blessed are ye that make peace, or the noises of peace
ye are the salt of the earth tumbling into pure water
remember the noise of empty bottles is greater

Blessed are ye that make peace, or the smiles of peace
you are the deadly nightshade in the kindergarten
you are the acid that's thrown into people's faces
you are the solar wind that castrates the blood
remember to keep smiling all the time

May the Lord lift his countenance upon thee
and give thee peace

May a big dog lift His leg upon thee
and piss hard upon thy shins

Peace is a picked flower
peace is words dying of sunshine
peace is a mahatma's unfinished masterpiece
peace breaks the hearts of the map-makers
peace is the chronic dystrophy of umpires

Peace is the agony of Aeschylus
stared at by women with shiny handbags and lorgnettes

Peace is giant orchids and oak-trees
growing out of the dirt in an undertaker's fingernails

Peace is the architect of war

More men die of peace than of war
geriatric hospitals stinking of half-dried urine
aren't the products of war

Peace is tiny

Peace is
Peace, peace, when there is no peace

      When there is no war
there's no true man and no no-man's land to satisfy
the addictions of the millionaire wilderness-builders

Peace is the assassin of heroes and this day
the white god of war is only a well-made dove
full of the fury of the Lord
poised in the smile of a Buddhist monk

One day it will become a crow whose claw exceeds
the hacksaw eye of the lammergeyer

Its teeth will drip sputum collected from the epileptic
tables of slanting conference rooms

Its mouth will bay with the rabies
drooled from the lips of speech-makers

It will spit upon the children in the street
and upon the assembly of young men together
and upon the popcorn generations
who pray for peace and go bowling the next morning

It will suck asthmas from the sun's last dragon
and wipe its mouth on the flowery red-guard
banners of those who demonstrate for peace only because
that's the way the wind blows

It will come mocking from the calibres of tear-gas guns
till they who sit down in front of embassies are scorched
naked as shaved wolves crying peace peace at the doors

It will lash the calm seas till their green backs bleed
and capsize the smug galleons of pilgrim fathers

It will warn the world of the ultimatums
droned in the bare-headed classrooms of Peking
and tell men of the military toys
sold in the glittering department stores of Dallas

Ideograms of war can be found
painted on walls anywhere where there are two people
drifting no more than a stone's throw apart

And the white-god dove of war will say

He that is without sin among you
let him be the first to cast a stone

god into my eyes and then you shall have
peace *when I'm dead and gone, mither,*
when I'm dead and gone

Damned are the men that mourn
for their cries interrupt the counterpoint of invisible guns

Damned are the meek
for they murmur about the discomfort of tinned sardines

Damned are they that hunger and thirst
for they can't throw hand-grenades or shout commands

Damned are the pure in heart
for all they can do is polish brass doorknobs on weekdays

Damned are they that have been persecuted
for they think martyrdom's the grandest eyrie in the mountains

Damned are the peacemakers
for they have condemned war when there is no way
to terminate the decisions of guns till they have
picked up the whole round world in their hands
and with a clean white cloth
wiped off the lands and seas

Conclusion

The children holding hands in the greenwood will never know
the orange horn impaling the sky behind the hunch-back
pines is a lurking ghoul pretending to be the moon rising

The man sitting on the gate near a smouldering signpost
points out the way with a steady finger notwithstanding
the endless nodding of his round head and mad-cow eyes

The distance is grey with ocean-history and the ceaseless
crying of storm-petrels, galleons and dolphin-sprees

Friendly horns croon along winding valley-roads and unseen
armies move on towards battlefields not yet chosen
their harlequin coats of arms as bright as the fractured
diamonds in their eyes reflecting the despair of campaigns

Forests of moss prosper upon the aged curves of boulders
and rain-kindled ferns overhang nine thousand steps
cut by goblin miners in a forgotten age when gold
ran in the blue veins of princes dreaming in castle halls

Lanterns among hills of innumerable jewels gleaming with tears
discover the long-lost cavern full of the broken promises of rainbows

And the last dragon on its back coiled in divine agony
offers its silken belly to sword or feather-duster and lies there
dying of uncontrollable laughter and a surfeit of greenhorn spells